SPELLING

5

SPELLING

by John Smith

5

CASSELL

Cassell Publishers Limited
Villiers House
41/47 Strand
London WC2N 5JE

©Cassell Publishers Ltd 1961 and 1986
Reprinted 1987, 1989, 1990, 1991, 1992

ISBN 0 304 31284 3

Typeset by Kalligraphics Ltd, Surrey

Printed and bound in Great Britain by
Hollen Street Press Limited, Slough, Berkshire

For Teachers and Parents

1. These books are designed to give children practice in spelling once or twice a day – when they come in from play, for instance.
2. Used only once a day, a child will go through this book five times and write 3,000 spellings in 'families' in the course of a school year.
3. Each page is a challenge to a child, as a crossword puzzle is to an adult, and should be presented in that light.
4. Correct spelling is all-important. The accurate writing of the answers is the main reason for doing the page; the solving of the clues is of secondary importance. An answer which is incorrectly spelt should be marked wrong.
5. If this book is used in the few minutes after play, scarcely any teaching time is taken up, and lessons begin quickly, quietly and purposefully.

For Girls and Boys

1. Number your page 1 to 15.
2. Read the clue; choose the word from the 'frame' which best fits the clue, and write it against the proper number.
3. Where two 'frame' words appear to fit the same clue, careful thought will show you that one of them is more suitable than the other. You can use a dictionary to help you choose the better one.
4. Only correctly spelt answers will be counted.

Contents

1. Amy Johnson was the first woman to fly — to Australia

2. Vesuvius is a —

3. A red fruit

4. A starchy food

5. The goods carried by a ship

6. An insect

7. A very brave person

8. Insects

9. The plural of potato

10. Ox-like animals

11. Very brave people

12. Mountains which erupt

13. Plural of tomato

14. Reflected sounds

15. A game

o

potato

mosquito

solo

volcano

hero

tomato

cargo

oes

echoes

buffaloes

mosquitoes

potatoes

tomatoes

heroes

volcanoes

dominoes

1. From another country

2. Animal of the cold lands

3. In space astronauts become —

4. 16×5

5. The sound made by a horse

6. Cargo

7. One who lives nearby

8. Male person left money or property in a will

9. Female person left money or property in a will

10. World War II was in the — of King George VI

11. The front part of the head

12. The finger next to the thumb

13. Man in charge of a group of people

14. Now here is the weather —

15. In the — of the painting was an old bridge

ei

eighty

neighbour

freight

weightless

reindeer

foreign

neigh

reign

heir

heiress

fore

forecast

foreman

forefinger

foreground

forehead

e̶ + ing

1. Hurting

2. Thrilling

3. Evading paying customs-duty

4. Having a belief

5. Saying 'No'

6. Drawing lines under

7. Eating dinner

8. Controlling a car

9. Glittering

10. Fleeing

11. Inspecting

12. Opposite of winning

13. Being joyful

14. Sweating

15. Astonishing

| exciting |
| underlining |
| surprising |
| driving |
| aching |
| examining |
| smuggling |
| perspiring |
| dining |
| sparkling |
| losing |
| believing |
| rejoicing |
| refusing |
| escaping |

1. A country

2. A boy's name

3. Rotate

4. Be very good at something

5. A fuel

6. A dog with drooping ears

7. An officer in the army

8. The — on the dress gave washing instructions

9. A dispute

10. A hard coating on teeth

11. Turning round and round

12. Starting

13. Smiling broadly

14. Opposite of losing

15. Tracy is — in the marathon next year

el

diesel oil

excel

colonel

quarrel

spaniel

Michael

enamel

label

Israel

swivel

nn

spinning

winning

running

grinning

beginning

1. An imaginary line around the centre of the earth

2. For keeping food cool

3. Better

4. Worse

5. An onlooker

6. A teacher often found in universities

7. Many TV sets can be moved about on —

8. An unmarried man

9. William I was the — of England

10. It provides warmth

11. A short-headed crocodile

12. Throws pictures on to a screen

13. Machine for making electricity

14. A person who governs

15. A moving staircase

or

projector

professor

escalator

conqueror

inferior

superior

bachelor

equator

alligator

governor

radiator

refrigerator

spectator

castors

generator

1. In a dangerous manner

2. At right angles to the horizon

3. In a serious manner

4. Opposite of rudely

5. Lastly

6. Completely

7. Nicola — goes skating on Saturdays

8. One at a time

9. Daintily

10. Beautiful

11. In a sincere manner

12. In a wise manner

13. In a strange manner

14. Correctly

15. At once

ly

finally

seriously

politely

usually

thoroughly

dangerously

vertically

wisely

immediately

sincerely

accurately

strangely

delicately

separately

lovely

y

1. Electricity made by water-power

2. Rubber part of a car wheel

3. A large snake

4. A sign for linking two words

5. A wind storm

6. Bulbs that will flower indoors in winter

7. Metal tower to carry power lines

8. Dictator

9. To do with cleanliness

10. The same sound in poetry

11. Used for causing explosions

12. A light gas

13. A secretary uses a —

14. Machine for making electric current

15. Energetic

typewriter

dynamo

dynamite

rhyme

python

tyre

hygiene

hyphen

cyclone

dynamic

pylon

hydrogen

tyrant

hyacinths

hydro-electricity

Shopping List

1. Green leaves eaten in salads
2. A dressing used on salads
3. Usually put into skins
4. Made from milk
5. Nuts
6. Dad likes milk — rather than plain
7. A fish
8. Used like butter
9. Crisp food often eaten with a cup of tea
10. Grain we eat
11. A long-stemmed vegetable
12. Made with oranges and sugar
13. Like a cabbage with a white head
14. A type of bread or flour
15. Dried fruit

marmalade

biscuits

mayonnaise

cauliflower

cereals

sausages

yogurt

currants

wholemeal

walnuts

margarine

chocolate

salmon

lettuce

celery

1. A law officer

2. Not easy

3. He did not want to — the customer

4. A long-necked animal

5. A Spring flower

6. Our new house is very — from the old one

7. The man was not — and made many mistakes

8. A fuel burnt in lamps and heaters

9. They gave us — to eat

10. Many a big car is driven by a —

11. Pulling

12. Appealing for money

13. We felt safe as the dog was — its tail

14. Turning the soil with a spade

15. Boasting

ff

paraffin

efficient

sheriff

sufficient

offend

different

chauffeur

difficult

giraffe

daffodil

gg

digging

begging

bragging

dragging

wagging

1. Quivering

2. Using the telephone

3. Dropping by parachute

4. The doctor was — her
    against whooping-cough

5. Lying in the sun

6. Crashing into each other

7. Making

8. A German river

9. A painful disease

10. A plant used for pies

11. A geometrical figure

12. A large evergreen shrub

13. Words sounding alike

14. Animal with a horn on its
     nose

15. Beat in music or verse

é + ing

parachuting

colliding

vibrating

sunbathing

telephoning

inoculating

manufacturing

rh

rhubarb

rhinoceros

Rhine

rhombus

rheumatism

rhododendron

rhythm

rhyme

1. Very fast trains

2. Daughters of kings and queens

3. Those who see an event

4. The fire destroyed both beds and —

5. Firms engaged in buying and selling

6. Roads taking heavy traffic from a city

7. Used for finding direction

8. This club is used by famous actors and —

9. The policeman took our names and —

10. They attend to the needs of aircraft passengers

11. Asim is—the cases on to the roof-rack

12. He fell whilst — his anorak

13. Stealing a person

14. Cutting

15. Taking part in worship

sses

princesses

addresses

mattresses

expresses

compasses

witnesses

by-passes

businesses

actresses

air-hostesses

pp

kidnapping

strapping

clipping

worshipping

unzipping

1. Much liked

2. Dad works at the — power station

3. For housing aircraft

4. Strange

5. A list of days and months

6. A sour liquid

7. Upright

8. Alike

9. He was a — visitor to our disco

10. Details

11. To do with the moon

12. Mum does not have — in her tea

13. A transparent material

14. A geometrical figure

15. A technical college

ar

vinegar

similar

peculiar

perpendicular

nuclear

regular

sugar

popular

calendar

lunar

hangar

particulars

poly

polytechnic
polygon
polythene

ed

1. Gave up the struggle
2. We — to the nine o'clock news
3. The Roman army — much of the known world
4. Burrowed underground
5. Afraid
6. Took a person's life
7. Vanished
8. The soldier climbed into his — car
9. The passengers — their seat belts
10. Sajid returned the library book he had —
11. Took place
12. Took off the cover
13. Possessing colour
14. The envelope was — quite clearly
15. Spoke in a very gentle voice

disappeared

tunnelled

uncovered

surrendered

listened

frightened

murdered

unfastened

coloured

whispered

addressed

armoured

borrowed

conquered

happened

1. Dreadful

2. In good supply

3. She takes one — of the medicine after meals

4. Having great power

5. Full of faith

6. His family were pleased with the — operation

7. As much as will go in a hand

8. Pleasing to the eye

9. Hoping for the best

10. In a graceful manner

11. Mt. Everest was climbed — in 1953

12. He was a — built man

13. In a faithful manner

14. In a manner pleasing to the eye

15. The climbers set out — on the ascent

ful

successful

hopeful

powerful

beautiful

handful

faithful

awful

spoonful

plentiful

fully

successfully

hopefully

gracefully

powerfully

faithfully

beautifully

1. Clothes for wearing in bed

2. A tree with 'winged' seeds

3. Beat in music or verse

4. A piece of music

5. A gas

6. A licence is not needed to ride a —

7. Oppression

8. A building for gymnastics

9. Strange

10. One of the Seven Wonders of the World

11. This rude behaviour was — of the man

12. The rabbit appeared to be — by the stoat

13. Tenderness towards someone in trouble

14. The land of the Pyramids

15. One who pretends to be better than he is

y

symphony

Pyramids

mysterious

rhythm

tyranny

gymnasium

pyjamas

sympathy

bicycle

sycamore

Egypt

typical

hypnotised

hypocrite

oxygen

1. Electricity is stored in a —

2. The reason for the crime remained a —

3. Monks live here

4. Nicola is three and goes to — school

5. Engineers are overhauling the —

6. Guns

7. Socks, tights and stockings department

8. A burial place

9. Diamonds and emeralds are types of —

10. Writing paper, etc.

11. Noon

12. Threatening

13. Only a few — remained unsold

14. The rock fell with a — noise

15. Icy roads can cause this

ery

jewellery

cemetery

mystery

monastery

stationery

hosiery

machinery

nursery

battery

artillery

dd

forbidding

oddments

midday

skidding

thudding

1. Valuable

2. A blow on the head can make you this

3. The noise of the traffic was —

4. Pleasant to eat

5. Spiteful

6. Distrustful

7. With lots of room

8. A goblin

9. The dog — the bone

10. Knotted and twisted

11. The man — his teeth in anger

12. Always does his best

13. Influenza is an — disease

14. Wary

15. He was — and never walked under ladders

cious

delicious

spacious

suspicious

atrocious

precious

unconscious

vicious

gn

gnashed

gnarled

gnawed

gnome

tious

superstitious

conscientious

infectious

cautious

Countries

1. The Pakistanis live in

2.   Turks

3.   Indians

4.   Afghans

5.   Finns

6.   Argentinians

7.   Egyptians

8.   Swiss

9.   Israelis

10.   Dutch

11.   Portuguese

12.   West Indians

West Indies

Egypt

Afghanistan

Pakistan

Switzerland

Holland

Finland

Argentina

India

Turkey

Israel

Portugal

CC

13. Found in an orchestra and played

14. Found in a car and pressed

15. Happen in dangerous places and to be avoided

piccolo

accidents

accelerator

1. 1000 make a metre

2. Sells precious stones

3. Used in the cure of disease

4. An underground room

5. Railway lines are — to each other

6. A very rich person

7. A sweet

8. Machine for moving earth

9. Protective clothing

10. Transparent wrapping material

11. Grub which changes into a butterfly

12. Made of wool

13. A picture

14. A plot of ground used as a garden

15. Precious stones, gold rings, etc.

II

lollipop

caterpillar

jeweller

jewellery

millimetres

bulldozer

allotment

millionaire

illustration

penicillin

cellar

overall

cellophane

woollen

parallel

1. One who takes photographs

2. A member of an army

3. A type of aircraft

4. Stores and processes information

5. It propels some types of aircraft

6. One who sells fruit

7. Introduces programmes on TV and radio

8. A boy's name

9. Does not have alcoholic drinks

10. One's personality

er

helicopter

propeller

teetotaller

Christopher

character

computer

soldier

announcer

photographer

fruiterer

11. A sugary top to a cake

12. Moving earth with a machine

13. The judge will be — them tomorrow

14. Using a gun

15. Overhauling a machine

é + ing

sentencing

servicing

icing

bulldozing

firing

1. Moved by machinery

2. Very wicked or devilish

3. In a — accident someone is killed

4. Exactly the same as

5. Fond of music

6. To do with history

7. In an orderly way

8. In a natural way

9. By experiment

10. By machinery

11. Deborah is — home by eight

12. Slowly

13. Completely

14. By accident

15. Not all Robin Hood's exploits are — true

al

identical

methodical

mechanical

diabolical

musical

fatal

historical

ally

historically

usually

naturally

mechanically

experimentally

gradually

totally

accidentally

1. Cannot be seen

2. She was in charge and — for our safety

3. Reasonable

4. Not possible

5. Can be heard

6. Horrible

7. Cannot be overcome

8. Can be made to bend

9. Beyond belief

10. Can be eaten

11. Her arm was aching and —

12. Best done with a hard brush

13. Weeping

14. Stealing

15. He was — his hands together

ible

impossible

audible

invincible

incredible

terrible

edible

sensible

invisible

flexible

responsible

bb

rubbing

scrubbing

throbbing

sobbing

robbing

1. To inflict pain

2. To make

3. A talk given to a class

4. A hole in a tyre

5. Tables, chairs, etc.

6. An introductory piece of music

7. To make prisoner

8. The writings of a country

9. The study of building

10. Degree of hotness

11. A broken bone

12. An aircraft

13. A spray

14. A display of clever flying

15. Our athletes go to an — class to keep fit

ture

overture

literature

puncture

temperature

torture

manufacture

furniture

architecture

fracture

lecture

capture

aero

aerobics

aerobatics

aerosol

aeroplane

1. Measures heat

2. Measures speed

3. Measures the fare in a taxi

4. Measures electric voltage

5. Measures a plane's height

6. Measures air pressure to see if it will be a fine day

7. I shall be pleased to — your kind invitation

8. Additional parts

9. Increase speed

10. Our visitor speaks English with a French —

11. In fog drivers must guard against —

12. 1/1000th part of a metre

13. 10 millimetres = 1 —

14. 100 centimetres = 1 —

15. 1000 metres = 1 —

meter

taximeter

voltmeter

altimeter

speedometer

barometer

thermometer

acc

accent

accidents

accessories

accept

accelerate

metre

metre

centimetre

millimetre

kilometre

1. A flower

2. The study of chemicals

3. There were four — in the play

4. When the birth of Jesus Christ is celebrated

5. A stage in the life of an insect

6. One who treats feet

7. A deep hole

8. The Christian faith

9. The train crash caused —

10. Ravinder loved singing and joined the — society

11. A member of a choir

12. A group of notes in music

ch

Christianity

Christmas

choral

chasm

chemistry

chrysanthemum

chord

chiropodist

chorister

chaos

characters

chrysalis

13. Beautiful

14. The winner received a — for £100

15. Ugly

que

grotesque

picturesque

cheque

1. Books of word meanings

2. Goods vehicles

3. Coal-mines

4. Punishments

5. Buildings for pigs

6. Thefts

7. Places for experiments

8. Programmes depicting real life

9. Collections of books

10. Special days

11. We found the price in the —

12. Scoundrel

13. Secret plotting

14. A table of teams

15. A friend

y + ies

documentaries

libraries

lorries

dictionaries

penalties

collieries

anniversaries

laboratories

robberies

sties

gue

colleague

intrigue

rogue

catalogue

league

1. To go down

2. Fruit, etc. to end a meal

3. Cross out

4. The fire had — the shop

5. After much thought they came to a —

6. Cheat

7. The artist was starting to — a poster

8. He is — to pass the exam

9. Used for cleaning

10. On purpose

11. They play well and — to win

12. The news created great —

13. Of very fine quality

14. To go beyond a set limit

15. All agreed to go — Kelly

de

detergent

determined

design

deliberately

descend

dessert

deceive

delete

deserve

decision

destroyed

exc

except

exceed

excellent

excitement

Pursuits

1. Fishing with a rod, line and hook

2. Using a camera

3. The study of the stars

4. Unpaid acting

5. Study of ancient remains

6. Stamp collecting

7. Sailing

8. Designs in needlework

9. Running, jumping, hurdling, etc.

10. He was a collector of —

11. A type of unarmed combat

12. Climbing mountains

13. Exploring underground passages

14. Underwater swimming

15. His knowledge of — helped him to repair the radio

philately

mountaineering

embroidery

athletics

yachting

angling

karate

electronics

antiques

pot-holing

astronomy

photography

skin-diving

archaeology

amateur dramatics

Space

1. The course of a planet or satellite

2. Used for slowing down spacecraft

3. One who journeys into space

4. Clothing worn in space

5. An object which circles another

6. The shuttle rose up from the — pad

7. To throw away

8. A layer of air surrounding our planet

9. Setting fire to the rocket fuel

atmosphere

orbit

jettison

satellite

spacesuits

ignition

astronaut

retro-rocket

launch

ily

10. In a dainty manner

11. In a saucy manner

12. Neatly

13. In a busy manner

14. In a happy manner

15. Cautiously

happily

warily

daintily

tidily

busily

saucily

1. The sick man had no —
   for food
2. The boy had an operation
   for —
3. She wrote her — for the
   job
4. Her hairdressing — was
   cancelled
5. Clapping
6. We use delicate — in the
   lab.
7. To be grateful for
8. Being near to the right
   answer
9. He had the — of a wealthy
   man
10. Arrested

apparatus

application

appendicitis

appointment

appreciate

apprehended

approximately

appearance

applause

appetite

é + ing

11. Very cold
12. Taking exercise
13. Getting rid of
14. The judges were — the
    names of the winners
15. The ambulance began —
    the other vehicles

exercising

overtaking

announcing

eliminating

freezing

1. A metal covering for knights of old

2. They were on their best — for the school trip

3. A haven for ships

4. Gossip

5. A heavy rain

6. To receive a knighthood is a great —

7. Wit

8. Containing colour

9. A line joining opposite corners of a rectangle

10. Not curved

11. Railway lines are — to each other

12. Slanting

13. A line through the centre of a circle

14. From the centre of a circle to the circumference

15. Shape with opposite sides equal and parallel

our

rumour

downpour

behaviour

armour

coloured

harbour

honour

humour

Geometry

parallel

parallelogram

diagonal

straight

oblique

diameter

radius

1. Cannot be detected

2. Beyond belief

3. Fair

4. Cannot be done without

5. He settled down in a —
    armchair

6. Horrible

7. Friendly

8. Clever

9. A building added on

10. Chief church in a city

11. A mountain cottage in the
     Alps

12. A slaughterhouse

13. We go here for a meal

14. For the care of the sick
     and injured

15. In here cricketers wait their
     turn to bat

able

indispensable

abominable

undetectable

unbelievable

capable

amicable

comfortable

reasonable

Buildings

hospital

pavilion

abattoir

chalet

restaurant

cathedral

annexe

att

1. She had an — of hay fever

2. Beautiful

3. Strive

4. He — a rope to the car

5. The car park — gave Mum her change

6. A room at the top of a house

7. The student had the right — to his work

attic

attitude

attractive

attempt

attached

attendant

attack

un

8. Not satisfactory

9. Without work

10. Not equal

11. Not affected by

12. Out of the ordinary

13. Alone

14. Not confirmed by an official

15. Not known

unusual

unaffected

unemployed

unofficial

unaccompanied

unknown

unsatisfactory

unequal

Occupations

1. A doctor

2. Looks after a library

3. Supplies spectacles

4. Someone who does heavy manual work

5. Welcomes guests at a hotel

6. Skilled in using or repairing machines

7. Performs surgical operations

8. One who draws plans

9. Someone who works with computers

10. A telephone switchboard operator

11. The injection — the pain

12. To be very upset

13. A part

14. Carried in a pocket

15. A relative

---

draughtsman

telephonist

computer operator

physician

surgeon

labourer

librarian

mechanic

receptionist

optician

ie

niece

relieved

handkerchief

piece

grieve

1. A writer of plays

2. The garden had two fine
    — iron gates

3. He stood — his hands and
    was obviously very upset

4. The — of the plane was
    on fire

5. Squirm and wriggle

6. Very unhappy

7. The old letter was
    beautifully —

8. Lines on the face

9. A cover

10. A form of combat

11. The lifeboat headed for
    the scene of the —

12. Not necessary

13. Not noticed

14. Not neighbourly

15. Not natural

wr

handwritten

wrapper

wreckage

wrestling

wretched

writhe

playwright

shipwreck

wringing

wrought

wrinkles

un

unnoticed
unnatural
unnecessary
unneighbourly

1. For storing things in

2. The farmer dug up a — of
    gold coins in a field

3. Rough

4. A husky voice is said to
    be —

5. A boy or girl at a boarding
    school

6. All powerful

7. It was cold — it was sunny

8. Forever

9. Nearly

10. When the alarm was raised
     the building was — blazing

11. Thoughtless

12. A method of watering crops

13. Bad tempered

14. Not regular

15. Not religious

oar

boarder

coarse

hoard

cupboard

hoarse

al

almost

almighty

already

always

although

irr

irregular

irreligious

irrigation

irritable

irresponsible

Tricky Ones

1. They are dancing at the — tonight
2. A musical instrument
3. A vegetable
4. Assorted
5. The things one owns
6. Tina answered the — for a secretary
7. A place to stay
8. An officer
9. A sweet based on sugar and white of egg
10. A sea animal like a small whale
11. A huge animal with a horn on its nose
12. A reptile with a large shell
13. An African animal fond of rivers
14. A type of leopard
15. Travels in leaps in Australia

lieutenant

possessions

xylophone

advertisement

miscellaneous

cauliflower

meringue

discotheque

accommodation

Animals

cheetah

tortoise

rhinoceros

kangaroo

porpoise

hippopotamus

1. Muttered

2. He was — a job in the mine

3. Walked into

4. The pan of water — on the cooker

5. They roared away in a high — car

6. She wore a pretty — dress

7. A — walk can raise a lot of money

8. The block of flats — above the houses

---

9. Past tense of occur

10. Past tense of deter

11. Past tense of defer

12. Past tense of refer

13. Past tense of prefer

14. Past tense of stir

15. Her favourite actor — in the film

ed

flowered

powered

murmured

offered

entered

towered

simmered

sponsored

---

deferred

referred

occurred

starred

stirred

deterred

preferred

Tricky Ones

1. We eat this

2. A king, a queen, or a gold coin

3. Very unusual

4. The name of a famous sea

5. One seeks knowledge from this

6. People or vehicles one behind the other

7. Wears three stripes

8. A bunch of flowers

9. Not required

10. To turn head over heels

11. Secret planning

12. He found the change of plan most —

13. Being sorry

14. Placing

15. Failing to remember

sergeant

bouquet

somersault

spaghetti

extraordinary

unnecessary

sovereign

encyclopaedia

queue

Mediterranean

tt

putting

forgetting

plotting

regretting

upsetting

Geography

1. Country with the largest population

2. Ocean between Europe and America

3. Famous waterfalls on the American/Canadian border

4. Capital of Greece

5. Melbourne, Sydney and Perth are in this country

6. A famous rock

7. A city within the city of Rome

8. A famous building in India

9. The highest mountain in the world

10. Large desert in North Africa

11. Capital of India

12. The largest ocean

13. Capital of Japan

14. The area around the North Pole

15. The area around the South Pole

Delhi

Australia

China

Sahara

Atlantic

Everest

Tokyo

Arctic

Antarctic

Athens

Vatican

Gibraltar

Taj Mahal

Pacific

Niagara Falls